To grannies,
lots of lave
Rachel + Damen
x x x

FRANCIS FRITH'S

COTSWOLDS
REVISITED
PHOTOGRAPHIC MEMORIES

ROBIN BROOKS is a freelance writer who lives in Cheltenham. His work includes plays for Radio 4, newspaper and magazine features, books, video scripts and commercial copywriting. Robin writes regularly on local interest subjects for the *Gloucestershire Echo* and *Gloucester Citizen*.

FRANCIS FRITH'S
PHOTOGRAPHIC MEMORIES

COTSWOLDS
REVISITED

PHOTOGRAPHIC MEMORIES

ROBIN BROOKS

First published in the United Kingdom in 2003 by
Frith Book Company Ltd

Hardback Edition 2003
ISBN 1-85937-453-0

British Library Cataloguing in Publication Data

Photographic Memories - Cotswolds Revisited
Robin Brooks

Frith Book Company Ltd
Frith's Barn, Teffont,
Salisbury, Wiltshire SP3 5QP
Tel: +44 (0) 1722 716 376
Email: info@francisfrith.co.uk
www.francisfrith.co.uk

Printed and bound in Great Britain

Front Cover: **BOURTON-ON-THE-WATER,**
View from The Memorial c1955 B392074
Frontispiece: **BILBURY,** *Arlington Row c1960* B530023

*The colour-tinting is for illustrative purposes only, and is not intended to be
historically accurate*

AS WITH ANY HISTORICAL DATABASE THE FRITH ARCHIVE IS CONSTANTLY
BEING CORRECTED AND IMPROVED AND THE PUBLISHERS WOULD
WELCOME INFORMATION ON OMISSIONS OR INACCURACIES

CONTENTS

FRANCIS FRITH
VICTORIAN PIONEER

FRANCIS FRITH, founder of the world-famous photographic archive, was a complex and multi-talented man. A devout Quaker and a highly successful Victorian businessman, he was philosophic by nature and pioneering in outlook.

By 1855 he had already established a wholesale grocery business in Liverpool, and sold it for the astonishing sum of £200,000, which is the equivalent today of over £15,000,000. Now a very rich man, he was able to indulge his passion for travel. As a child he had pored over travel books written by early explorers, and his fancy and imagination had been stirred by family holidays to the sublime mountain regions of Wales and Scotland. 'What lands of spirit-stirring and enriching scenes and places!' he had written. He was to return to these scenes of grandeur in later years to 'recapture the thousands of vivid and tender memories', but with a different purpose. Now in his thirties, and captivated by the new science of photography, Frith set out on a series of pioneering journeys up the Nile and to the

Near East that occupied him from 1856 until 1860.

INTRIGUE AND EXPLORATION

These far-flung journeys were packed with intrigue and adventure. In his life story, written when he was sixty-three, Frith tells of being held captive by bandits, and of fighting 'an awful mid-night battle to the very point of surrender with a deadly pack of hungry, wild dogs'. Wearing flowing Arab costume, Frith arrived at Akaba by camel seventy years before Lawrence of Arabia, where he encountered 'desert princes and rival sheikhs, blazing with jewel-hilted swords'.

He was the first photographer to venture beyond the sixth cataract of the Nile. Africa was still the mysterious 'Dark Continent', and Stanley and Livingstone's historic meeting was a decade into the future. The conditions for picture taking confound belief. He laboured for hours in his wicker dark-room in the sweltering heat of the desert, while the volatile chemicals fizzed dangerously in their trays. Back in London he exhibited his photographs and was 'rapturously cheered' by members of the Royal Society. His reputation as a photographer was made overnight.

VENTURE OF A LIFE-TIME

Characteristically, Frith quickly spotted the opportunity to create a new business as a specialist publisher of photographs. He lived in an era of immense and sometimes violent change.

For the poor in the early part of Victoria's reign work was exhausting and the hours long, and people had precious little free time to enjoy themselves. Most had no transport other than a cart or gig at their disposal, and rarely travelled far beyond the boundaries of their own town or village. However, by the 1870s the railways had threaded their way across the country, and Bank Holidays and half-day Saturdays had been made obligatory by Act of Parliament. All of a sudden the working man and his family were able to enjoy days out and see a little more of the world.

With typical business acumen, Francis Frith foresaw that these new tourists would enjoy having souvenirs to commemorate their days out. In 1860 he married Mary Ann Rosling and set out on a new career: his aim was to photograph every city, town and village in Britain. For the next thirty years he travelled the country by train and by pony and trap, producing fine photographs of seaside resorts and beauty spots that were keenly bought by millions of Victorians. These prints were painstakingly pasted into family albums and pored over during the dark nights of winter, rekindling precious memories of summer excursions.

THE RISE OF FRITH & CO

Frith's studio was soon supplying retail shops all over the country. To meet the demand he gathered about him a small team of photographers, and published the work of independent artist-photographers of the calibre of Roger Fenton and Francis Bedford. In order to gain some understanding of the scale of Frith's business one only has to look at the catalogue issued by Frith & Co in 1886: it runs to some 670 pages, listing not only many thousands of views of the British Isles but also many photographs of most European countries, and China, Japan, the USA and Canada - note the sample page shown on page 9 from the hand-written Frith & Co ledgers recording the pictures. By 1890 Frith had created the greatest specialist photographic publishing company in the world, with over 2,000 sales outlets - more than the combined number that Boots and WH Smith have today! The picture on the next page shows the Frith & Co display board at Ingleton in the Yorkshire Dales (left of window). Beautifully constructed with a mahogany frame and gilt inserts, it could display up to a dozen local scenes.

POSTCARD BONANZA

The ever-popular holiday postcard we know today took many years to develop. In 1870 the Post Office issued the first plain cards, with a pre-printed stamp on one face. In 1894 they allowed other publishers' cards to be sent through the mail with an attached adhesive halfpenny stamp. Demand grew rapidly, and in 1895 a new size of postcard was permitted called the court card, but there was little room for illustration. In 1899, a year after Frith's death, a new card measuring 5.5 x 3.5 inches became the standard format, but it was not until 1902 that the divided back came into being, so that the address and message could be on one face and a full-size illustration on the other. Frith & Co were in the vanguard of postcard development: Frith's sons Eustace and Cyril continued their father's monumental task, expanding the number of views offered to the public and recording more and more places in Britain, as the coasts and countryside were opened up to mass travel.

Francis Frith had died in 1898 at his villa in Cannes, his great project still growing. The archive he created continued in business for another seventy years. By 1970 it contained over a third of a million pictures showing 7,000 British towns and villages.

FRANCIS FRITH'S LEGACY

Frith's legacy to us today is of immense significance and value, for the magnificent archive of evocative photographs he created provides a unique record of change in the cities, towns and villages throughout Britain over a century and more. Frith and his fellow studio photographers revisited locations many times down the years to update their views, compiling for us an enthralling and colourful pageant of British life and character.

We are fortunate that Frith was dedicated to recording the minutiae of everyday life. For it is this sheer wealth of visual data, the painstaking chronicle of changes in dress, transport, street layouts, buildings, housing, engineering and landscape that captivates us so much today. His remarkable images offer us a powerful link with the past and with the lives of our ancestors.

THE VALUE OF THE ARCHIVE TODAY

Computers have now made it possible for Frith's many thousands of images to be accessed almost instantly. Frith's images are increasingly used as visual resources, by social historians, by researchers into genealogy and ancestry, by architects and town planners, and by teachers involved in local history projects.

In addition, the archive offers every one of us an opportunity to examine the places where we and our families have lived and worked down the years. Highly successful in Frith's own era, the archive is now, a century and more on, entering a new phase of popularity. Historians consider the Francis Frith Collection to be of prime national importance. It is the only archive of its kind remaining in private ownership. Francis Frith's archive is now housed in an historic timber barn in the beautiful village of Teffont in Wiltshire. Its founder would not recognize the archive office as it is today. In place of the many thousands of dusty boxes containing glass plate negatives and an all-pervading odour of photographic chemicals, there are now ranks of computer screens. He would be amazed to watch his images travelling round the world at unimaginable speeds through internet lines.

The archive's future is both bright and exciting. Francis Frith, with his unshakeable belief in making photographs available to the greatest number of people, would undoubtedly approve of what is being done today with his lifetime's work. His photographs depicting our shared past are now bringing pleasure and enlightenment to millions around the world a century and more after his death.

THE COTSWOLDS REVISITED

AN INTRODUCTION

MILLIONS OF TOURISTS who visit Britain each year put the Cotswolds at the top of their 'must see' list. Tourists apart, the region is a haven of picturesque peace and timeless tranquillity. But in centuries gone by this region was an economic powerhouse, one of the most thriving agricultural and industrial parts of the country.

The name Cotswolds originally applied only to the area immediately around the source of the River Windrush, but the area expanded to embrace the whole sheep-rearing region. 'Cots' referred to a place where sheep were kept, and 'wolds' meant hills (although some say that the area was named after a Saxon warlord named Cod).

From the 14th century onwards, wool merchants hereabouts built their wealth on a breed of sheep known as the Cotswold Lion, developed by selective breeding from the Logwool, which was brought to Britain by the Romans. Cotswold Lions were so named because it was traditional at shear-

BROADWAY, *High Street c1955* B222048

10

ing time to leave the forelocks and head unshaved, so the animal appeared to have a mane. Though now a rare breed, the Cotswold Lion remains the biggest domestic sheep in Britain.

Wool produced on the hills was woven into cloth in Cotswold villages. At first this was a domestic industry, and the top-half-open, bottom-half-closed front doors to be found in Winchcombe and elsewhere are a reminder of those times - wool spinners and weavers went about their business with the door half open so that passing merchants could inspect the quality of their work.

Later, mechanisation replaced home workers, and woollen mills were established in places such as Stroud, where plenty of fast streams provided the energy to power machinery. Woollen cloth produced in Stroud was considered the best in the world, and it was in great demand in Britain and abroad. The Guards' red uniforms were traditionally made from Stroud cloth, and in pre-Reformation times the Pope wore robes made from cloth woven here.

It was wool that financed the magnificent 'cathedrals of the Cotswolds'. Market towns such as Northleach, Winchcombe and Cirencester boast churches that were always far grander and larger than was warranted by the local communities. But these great perpendicular lanterns of light were an expression of affluence on the part of the super-rich merchants who stumped up the funds to build them (and who also hoped they were buying a place in heaven).

Cotswold stone roofs are characteristic of the region. Because this was sheep-rearing country, little land was given over to arable agriculture, so there was not much straw for thatching purposes. Limestone slates were the time-honoured alternative - the Roman villas at Chedworth, Winchcombe and Whitcombe were all roofed in Cotswold stone. Quarries such as those at Guiting and Eyford, near Stow, did a roaring trade in the supply of roofing tiles. The best stone for the purpose is called Pendal, which is found at a depth of about eight feet. In times gone by this was quarried in October, then left to

STROUD, *King Street 1900* 45733

over-winter so that frost could season the stone. The following spring the limestone was split into layers from which the tiles were shaped.

The Cotswolds' past harbours some surprises. Back in the days of Charles II, for example, Winchcombe was a hot bed of insurrection and a place of revolt: the reason was tobacco. Not many years after tobacco was introduced to Britain from America by the pirate Sir John Hawkins, the entrepreneurial farmers of Winchcombe discovered that the local soil and micro climate produced excellent conditions for growing the fragrant weed. Fortunes were made by its cultivation, and for a time tobacco rivalled the wool trade as the Cotswolds' major money-spinner. By the time of Charles II, Gloucestershire-grown tobacco was seen as a threat to trade by growers in the Virginia colonies on the other side of the Atlantic. The Crown exchequer levied a duty on imported tobacco, while the home-produced variety contributed nothing to the coffers. Consequently tobacco growing in Britain was banned. The people of Winchcombe petitioned the king, but when His Majesty rejected their plea they carried on growing tobacco anyway. Enraged by such flagrant disobedience, the monarch despatched his Life Guard from London to seek out and destroy the banned baccy. The crack troops arrived - and were soon driven off by the people of Winchcombe. Next, a troop of soldiers from Gloucester was ordered to burn the illegal crop. But they were met by 500 locals, who pointed pistols, brandished whatever weapons were to hand and threatened to kill both the men and the horses they rode if the soldiers so much as bruised one of the precious leaves.

After that, Winchcombe was left well alone. Before long, however, the sheer volume of tobacco being imported from the colonies as the trade became highly organised meant that demand for home-grown weed diminished. The only reminder of Winchcombe's one-time trade is in the name 'Tobacco Close' - a road on the left as you enter the town after descending Cleeve Hill.

CIRENCESTER, *Market Place 1898* 40964

Not far from Winchcombe is Hayles Abbey. It is now no more than an impressive ruin, but until the Reformation the Cistercian monastery was home to a relic much revered by medieval trippers. The item in question was a phial said to contain blood that dripped from the body of Christ as he was crucified.

Yew trees are often found in Cotswold churchyards, most famously in the churchyard of St Mary's, Painswick. Some are shaped like field mushrooms, others are plump and rounded; there are cones and orbs, upright box-shapes and dumpy bap-like trees, but the most important thing about the yews is their number: there are 99. According to local lore, it is impossible to round their number up to 100. Every time one is planted, another dies, so the churchyard remains - like a nervous cricketer - forever one short of its century. Most of the cleverly-clipped trees were saplings in 1800. Some say yews were favoured because they are evergreen and live to a ripe old age, thus symbolising immortality. But there may also be truth in the view that English longbows were made of yew, so growing them provided the parson with a handy cash crop.

Despite the traffic that perpetually trundles along its main street, Painswick is as pretty as the lid of a chocolate box. Painswick's rural tranquillity suffered a cruel blow during the Second World War, when in the early morning of 12 June 1941 bombs rained down on the village. Four homes were destroyed in the raid, seven suffered serious damage, and a further 35 had windows blown in, or tiles blown off the roof. Ten people were injured in the bombings, and two children were killed; both of them, by a sad irony, were evacuees who had been billeted in Painswick for their own safety.

According to the various travel brochures, Bourton on the Water is billed as either 'the Queen of the Cotswolds', 'the Venice of the Cotswolds', or 'the jewel in the Cotswolds' crown'. The village sits at the confluence of a number of ancient routes, most important of which is the Fosse Way (less romantically known as the A429). This Roman road runs

FAIRFORD, *Croft House, The Croft 1948* F145016

from the mouth of the River Humber in the north-east of England to Devon in the south-west, so you could say that Bourton has been on the tourist route for thousands of years. It was in the mid-19th century, however, that visitors began to arrive in large numbers. Then, in the latter years of Victoria's reign, bicycling boomed in popularity and increased the influx of weekenders to Bourton, as men and women explored the new-found independence of two-wheeled pedal power. The Old New Inn catered for cyclists, offering refreshments and overnight accommodation. It was behind this pub in the 1930s that a Mr Morris, helped by a few friends, built the famous model village. This 1/9th scale reproduction of Bourton opened for public viewing on the same day that George VI was crowned king in 1937.

'Stow on the Wold where the wind blows cold' is a well-known local adage. That wind has done much to shape Stow. Sitting on the Roman Fosse Way, 800 feet up on a rounded tump, the surrounding landscape was excellent sheep country. Wool merchants thrived and built themselves fine houses in Stow, and used their wealth to fund the building of the parish church of St Edward. The heart of Stow is its Square, where stalls were first set up for the Thursday market (which continues to this day) in 1107. The cross in the middle of the Square is not as old as that, but it is ancient, erected as a reminder to medieval traders that they should not try to pull the wool they were selling over their customers' eyes. On its shaft is an eloquent brass plaque that reports: 'This ancient cross was restored in 1875 to commemorate the munificence of the late Joseph Chamberlayn, Chamberlayn and squire of Maugersbury Manor house who in addition to many other benevolent acts gave two thousand pounds to obtain a supply of pure water for this parish'. Fine man. Squeezed between the buildings in Stow's

ASCOTT-UNDER-WYCHWOOD, *The Green c1950* A140003

Square are alleys, known locally as tures. These follow the patterns of old burgage strips, and on market days in times gone by, sheep were driven in single file along these narrow ways to be counted.

No strangers to Stow in their time were Tom, Dick and Harry - three brothers with the surname Dunston - who were Gloucestershire's most notorious highwaymen. They were in business during the latter half of the 18th century, and plied their trade in nearby Wychwood Forest. The trio rose to infamy by holding up the Gloucester to Oxford stage coach, a heist that bagged them hundreds of pounds. But less lucky was their attempt to burgle Tangley Manor, between Stow and Burford. The household had been tipped off, and laid a trap. When Dick put his hand through the grille in the front door to unlatch the lock, his arm was noosed and held fast. Rather than let him be caught, Dick's brothers lopped his arm off. Not surprisingly, Dick

gave up highway robbery after this mishap, though his brothers continued in the thieving business until 1784, when they unsuccessfully tried to shoot the landlord of an inn. The bullet bounced off the innkeeper's money belt, which saved his life; in the commotion that followed, the local constabulary arrived and apprehended Tom and Harry, who were hanged in Gloucester.

Cirencester is another celebrated market town in the region - in fact it is one of the oldest market towns in the country. The Romans, who called the town Corinium, built a new market in the 2nd century, so there must have been an even earlier one. An agricultural market is mentioned in *Domesday*, and by the 14th century the goods on offer included livestock, dairy foods, fish, salt, alum, textiles, lead, tin and brass. In the following centuries the town became a centre for the wool and weaving industries, and the merchants who grew rich by these trades helped to fund the magnificent church of St John the Baptist - one of the

CHARLBURY, *Sheep Street c1950* C444008

largest parish churches in the country.

Just inside Worcestershire is Broadway, sometimes described as the prettiest village in England. For the many visitors it attracts, Broadway is a self-fulfilling prophecy of the Cotswolds, with its handsome houses in honey-hued stone, a village green shaded by spreading chestnuts, pints of foaming ale in oak-beamed inns and Earl Grey in the afternoons. Tranquil though it is now, back in the 17th century Broadway was a thriving staging post, and horse-drawn carriages by the dozen stopped to feed and water en route from London to Worcester - a journey of 17 hours. Over 30 inns offered passengers refreshment and accommodation. This lucrative trade came to a close with the arrival of the railway, which enabled the surrounding countryside to be developed as one of the country's most important market gardening areas.

A local landmark is Broadway Tower. This 65 feet tall frippery stands on top of Fish Hill, and was built in the 18th century by the 6th Earl of Coventry to try and alleviate his new bride's homesickness. Her family lived at Croom Court near Worcester, and she had the idea that it might be possible to see her former home from the top of Fish Hill. To test the point, a beacon was lit: sure enough, her mother and father in Croom Court could see their daughter's bonfire. In an effort to please her, the earl had Broadway Tower built so that whenever home pangs tugged at Mrs Coventry's heart, she could climb to the top of the folly and weep towards Worcester. William Morris, the designer, poet, painter and social reformer, spent long holidays living in Broadway Tower, and so did his fellow Pre-Raphaelites Edward Burne-Jones and Dante Gabriel Rossetti. No doubt they found the view from the top an inspiration - it overlooks 13 counties.

CIRENCESTER *1898* 40982

Like all self-respecting villages hereabouts, Broadway has ghosts galore. One of the least coy is that of a woman, who, it is said, was killed in times of yore when out hunting. She trots her spectral route along White Ladies Lane at the top end of the village quite regularly, so people will tell you.

It is curious that the ancient former parish church of St Eadburgha stands in isolation about a mile out of Broadway. It is now open to visitors from April to October, but since 1839 members of the congregation have not had to walk so far for evensong. In that year St Michael and All Angels' church opened just round the corner from the village green. It is not a particularly attractive church building, in stark contrast to so many others in the Cotswolds - but it makes a change.

WOODCHESTER, *The Church 1900* 45593

THE COTSWOLDS

CHELTENHAM, *The Promenade 1901* 47262

Neptune's Fountain was designed by the borough engineer Joseph Hall. Modelled on Rome's Fontana di Trevi and carved from Portland stone by the local firm of R L Boulton, this first gushed on 30 October 1893. It commemorates nothing, and is in memory of nobody; it was part of a general scheme to perk up the Promenade.

CHELTENHAM
High Street 1906 54320

Trams first trundled down Cheltenham's streets on 22 August 1901. By the end of the 1920s they had been rendered redundant by the quicker, go-anywhere buses, and the trams were withdrawn in 1930. The High Street is the original part of Cheltenham. On old maps the name Cheltenham Street appears, because until the building boom of the Spa years there was little more of the town than this.

▼ **CHELTENHAM,** *The Queen's Hotel 1901* 47269

The Queen's Hotel was built in 1837 at a cost of £47,000. The 70-bedroom hotel has been a temporary home to a glittering array of notables including Prince Louis Jerome Napoleon, the Rajah of Sarawak and the Prince of Wales, later Edward VII. During World War II the American Services Club took up residence here.

▶ **CHELTENHAM**
The Promenade 1907
59033

The building to the left with stone columns at its entrance was once home to a painter named Millet. Later it became the Imperial Hotel, and then in 1856 it was the Imperial Club for 'resident noblemen and gentlemen'. From 1874 until 1987 this was Cheltenham's main post office, and today it is a department store.

◄ **CHELTENHAM**
*The College
Ground 1907*
59039A

Cheltenham hosts the
longest-established
annual first-class
cricket festival in the
world. The first
'cricket week' at the
College ground (it was
not called a festival
until 1906) was
organised by James
Lillywhite, the College
coach, in 1878, and
cost £120 to stage.

► **CHELTENHAM**
*The Winter
Gardens 1923* 73495

Cheltenham's own
Crystal Palace stood in
Imperial Gardens. It
was built in 1879 to a
design by J T Darby,
with the intended
purpose of providing 'a
large concert room and
other accessories,
calculated to afford
recreation and
amusement to the
upper classes.' It was
demolished in
September 1940.

CHELTENHAM
The Promenade 1931
83804

Originally known as the
Sherborne, or Imperial
Promenade, Cheltenham's
fashionable thoroughfare
began its existence as a
walkway from the High
Street to a spa pump room
that stood where the
Queen's Hotel now stands.
The Prom, as it is known in
the town, was laid out
properly in 1818 and lined
with 44 chestnut trees.

► CHELTENHAM
The Strand 1937
87923

Next door to Gillhams' gifts and stationery shop (left) is the Cadena Cafe with its first-floor oriel window, which opened at the turn of the 20th century. Over on the right is an onion and dragon lamp standard designed by the borough engineer Joseph Hall, who was also responsible for Neptune's fountain in the Prom. These street lamps appeared in 1897.

◄ CIRENCESTER
Market Place 1898
40964

Cirencester was known as Corinium in Roman times, when it was the second largest settlement in England. It has always been an important market town for the surrounding predominantly agricultural area; this view shows the Market Place.

▲ **CIRENCESTER** *1898* 40982

The parish church of St John the Baptist overlooks the town. This magnificent building dates from the 12th century, and the splendid tower was built in the early 15th century. Inadequate foundations meant that the tower began to show signs of instability even before it was completed, and it had to be shored up with spur buttresses.

◄ **CIRENCESTER**
The Barracks 1898
40983

Also known locally as the Armoury, this castellated building stands at the entrance to Cirencester Park and was built in 1856. The building was once the HQ of the 4th Battalion of the Gloucestershire Regiment.

CIRENCESTER
*Gloucester Street
1898* 42363

Cirencester has managed to keep the worst ravages of unsympathetic development at bay. Most of the buildings shown in this picture, which was taken in the latter years of Queen Victoria's reign, can be seen in Gloucester Street to this day. The boys in their Sunday best were plainly fascinated by the photographer.

CIRENCESTER, *Castle Street c1955* C106008

Castle Street takes its name from the fortification, probably Norman, that stood hereabouts. After being sacked in 1142 it was rebuilt, only to be destroyed again by order of Henry III in 1216.

CIRENCESTER, *Black Jack Street c1955* C106009

Daniel George Bingham, a great benefactor to the town, was born in Black Jack Street in 1830. The building with the wide archway on the right was demolished some years ago to make way for the Royal Mail delivery office.

► **CIRENCESTER**
Dyer Street c1955
C106023

Cirencester's meandering street pattern developed in medieval times, a departure from the regimented grid system of Roman times. On the right, the building with the oriel window above the entrance is Bingham House, built in 1905 as the town library.

◄ **BROADWAY**
The Tower c1955
B222064

This local landmark stands on Fish Hill. Broadway Tower is a 65 feet high folly built in the 18th century by the 6th Earl of Coventry. On a clear day, 13 counties can be seen from the Gothic battlements.

▲ **BROADWAY,** *The Lygon Arms 1899* 44109

One of the oldest hotels in the country, The Lygon Arms boasts a 14th-century fireplace set into its 4 feet thick walls. During the Civil War, the hotel provided accommodation in 1645 for Charles I and his Cavaliers, and then in 1651 for Oliver Cromwell and his Roundheads.

◀ **BROADWAY**
High Street 1955
B222062

Until the 1990s, Broadway High Street was home to the Gordon Russell furniture factory. Gordon Russell himself literally set the standard by which all British furniture was made in the 1940s, as he chose the designs and approved the specification for Utility furniture, the only kind that could be made in the country during the Second World War.

▼ **BROADWAY,** *High Street c1955* B222048

From about 1600 Broadway was a thriving staging post, and horse-drawn carriages by the dozen stopped here to feed and water en route from London to Worcester - a journey of more than 17 hours. Over 30 inns offered passengers refreshment and accommodation.

► **BROADWAY**
The Village 1899 44108

Broadway is mentioned in the *Domesday Book*. It was owned by the Benedictine abbey of nearby Pershore until the Dissolution of the Monasteries by Henry VIII. Notice the oil lamp standard in the foreground of this late Victorian photograph.

◄ **BROADWAY**
The Village 1899
44111

The harrow on the grass verge reminds us that the surrounding Vale of Evesham was, and remains to this day, a major agricultural region. More (and many say the best) asparagus is grown here than anywhere else in the country. Locals call it 'gras'.

▶ **BOURTON-ON-THE-WATER**
Memorial Corner
c1955 B392072

'At weekends in summer and on Bank Holidays, Bourton on the Water has to suffer the invasions which have resulted from the discovery of its beauty, but at other times its charms are unobscured and can be more fully appreciated'. So reads a local guide book of 1924 - and the words are as apt now as they were then.

BOURTON-ON-THE-WATER
Harrington House c1955 B392041

The village is blessed with fine country houses as well as more modest cottages, built from locally quarried stone that has mellowed to the colour of honey on butter. Few buildings date back further than the 17th century, and Harrington House is one of the oldest.

BOURTON-ON-THE-WATER, *The View from the Memorial c1955* B392074

The village sits at the confluence of a number of ancient routes, the most important of which is the Fosse Way. This Roman road runs from the mouth of the River Humber in the north-east of England to Devon in the south-west. So you could say that it has been on the tourist route for thousands of years.

BOURTON-ON-THE-WATER
The River Windrush c1965
B392126

In various travel guides, Bourton is billed as either 'the Queen of the Cotswolds', 'the jewel in the Cotswolds' crown', or 'the Venice of the Cotswolds'.

BOURTON-ON-THE-WATER, *The Bridge c1955* B392067

Five bridges span the River Windrush in the village. The most recent commemorates the coronation of Queen Elizabeth II in 1953. Bourton's oldest bridge dates from 1754, and stands in front of the old Corn Mill, which opened in 1978 as the Cotswold Motor Museum.

BOURTON-ON-THE-WATER
The Model Village c1955 B392050

Behind The Old New Inn, a Mr Morris - helped by a few friends - built the famous model village in the 1930s. This one-ninth scale reproduction of Bourton opened for public viewing on the same day that George VI was crowned king in 1937.

BISLEY, *The Seven Springs c1955* B110002

The carved inscription above the spouting water reads 'Bless ye the Lord, praise him and magnify.' Long before Christianity, springs were attributed with a spiritual significance. In pagan times the number seven was of special superstitious importance, and examples of Seven Springs are found at other places in the Cotswolds.

CLEEVE HILL
The Golf Club House c1955
C115004

The Cotswold Hills Golf Club was founded in 1902 by Harold Webb, who owned a brickworks in Cheltenham. In 1909 the former Prime Minister Arthur Balfour accepted the club's invitation to play at the course. The club house we see here opened in 1938.

CLEEVE HILL, *The Golf Course 1907* 59056

The golf course was a great success, attracting a membership of over 100 in the first year. Contributing to this popularity was the electric tram service that ran to the top of the hill from Cheltenham and opened in 1901.

CLEEVE HILL, *The Quarry 1907* 59059

Oolitic limestone has been quarried at Cleeve Hill for centuries. In days gone by it was called 'freestone' because it was relatively easy to obtain and work.

CLEEVE HILL
View to the Malvern Hills 1931 83822

Cleeve Hill rises to an altitude of 1,000 feet, and is topped by common land that occupies a plateau of 2,000 acres. From the escarpment there are views across the vale to the Malvern Hills and the Severn Estuary.

CLEEVE HILL, *The Rising Sun Hotel c1960* C115046

Though it has been added to in recent decades, the Rising Sun Hotel is easily recognisable from this photograph of 40 years ago. It has long been a popular venue with the racing fraternity.

► **HAILES ABBEY**
From the East 1924
76165

These overgrown ruins are the remains of a Cistercian abbey that once attracted pilgrims by the thousand in medieval times. They came to a shrine that was said to contain a phial of Christ's blood. Today the area continues to attract large numbers of people, but now they are drawn by pick-your-own fruit farms.

◄ **NORTHLEACH**
The Green c1960
N125031

This Cotswold town has much in common with other old wool towns to the north and south of it, such as Chipping Campden and Cirencester. The magnificent 15th-century church, dedicated to St Peter and St Paul, was funded by local merchants. Some of their stories are told in the church's notable collection of brasses.

▲ **NORTHLEACH,** *The Stocks c1955* N125006

The stocks and pillory in Market Square remind us of a time when justice was swift and direct. Northleach stands on the road from South Wales to London, and so it became an important coaching town where inns such as the half-timbered Kings Head on the left provided shelter and accommodation to passengers.

◄**NORTHLEACH**
Market Place c1960
N125016

Until the by-pass opened in the 1990s, Northleach High Street was chock-a-block with heavy traffic. Today the scene is more reminiscent of this peaceful scene from the past. Most of the buildings in the town centre date from Tudor and Jacobean days.

NORTHLEACH
Market Square
c1955 N125013

Within a short walk of the Market Square are two interesting museums. One is devoted to a working display of mechanical music machines, the other - housed in a former prison - is the Countryside Collection.

PAINSWICK, *New Street and the War Memorial c1960* P3021

Most of the cleverly clipped yew trees in the churchyard were saplings in 1800. According to local legend, they number 99. The story goes that every time an extra one is planted, an existing one dies, so the churchyard remains like a nervous batsman forever one short of its century.

PAINSWICK, *The Church 1900* 45597

St Mary's church is the focus of this ancient little town, which is built almost exclusively from Cotswold stone. The church tower houses a peal of twelve bells. In the tiny square nearby are the town's unusual stocks, made from iron.

PAINSWICK, *The Lychgate c1955* P3015

Although it looks much older, the lychgate into the churchyard was built only a century ago. Its apparent antiquity stems from the fact that its timbers were taken from the former bell frame. If we look up towards the gable, we will see that the bargeboards are decorated with carved bells.

44

PAINSWICK
General View 1901 47361

Painswick was a market centre for the smaller villages along the valley. It had its characters, such as Percy-from-Painswick, mentioned by Laurie Lee, author of *Cider With Rosie*, who grew up in nearby Slad.

PAINSWICK, *High Street c1960* P3024

In 1905 the world opened up to isolated villagers when a motor bus service from Stroud to Painswick was started by the Great Western Railway. Prior to the public opening, local dignitaries were invited on a trial run aboard the Daimler bus to Painswick, where they took lunch in The Falcon (right) before the journey back.

PAINSWICK
The Village c1960
P3026

In September the annual Clipping ceremony takes place in Painswick, as it has done for centuries. It has nothing to do with pruning the trees, but derives from the Saxon word 'clyppan', meaning 'to embrace'. At the ceremony villagers gather in the churchyard, hold hands, and form a circle round the church while singing hymns.

PAINSWICK, *Bisley Street c1960* P3027

Most buildings are of the limestone that has for many years been quarried from nearby Painswick Beacon, so the town sits comfortably on the ground from which it comes.

PAINSWICK
Gloucester Road
c1960 P3028

In times gone by there was great rivalry and mistrust between the people of Painswick and their neighbours in Stroud, just a few miles away. It is said that Stroud people would never accept food in Painswick because they believed people there ate 'bow-wow' pie - made from stray dogs!

PRESTBURY, *The Burgage c1960* P112021

In the late 1970s, Tom Graveney, the Gloucestershire, Worcestershire and England cricketer, was landlord of The Royal Oak Inn (left). A fine and stylish batsman, he played in 79 tests and scored 4,482 runs including 11 centuries. He was awarded the OBE for services to cricket in 1968.

▼ **PRESTBURY,** *The Burgage c1955* P112022

The word 'burgage' is an old legal term referring to a plot of land in a town for which a tenant paid a yearly rent in money or service to the landlord. This tucked-away quarter of the village has changed little since this photograph was taken.

► **PRESTBURY**
The Kings Arms c1960
P112016

Fred Archer, one of the most successful jockeys of all time, lived in Prestbury, and his father was landlord of The Kings Arms. In a short career Fred Archer had 2,148 wins from 8,004 rides, but his life was beset with personal tragedies, and he committed suicide at the age of 29.

◄ **PRESTBURY**
High Street c1955
P112015

Until the 1930s, trams ran along Prestbury High Street en route to the top of Cleeve Hill. A workman was employed to grease the rails at the sharp bend just out of sight in the distance. This prevented the outside wheel on its solid axle juddering as the tram took the corner. No doubt passengers were grateful for the greaser's efforts.

► **PRESTBURY**
Bouncers Lane and Blacksmith's Lane c1960 P112018

This thatched cottage stands between Bouncers Lane and Blacksmith's Lane, and is one of many half-timbered buildings in the village. Prestbury claims to be the most haunted village in Gloucestershire. Among the many spectral figures is a cavalier: it is said that he was executed by the staunchly Parliamentarian people of Prestbury in the Civil War.

PRESTBURY
Deep Street c1960
P112019

Peeking over the roof of the bow-fronted pharmacy is the castellated tower of St Mary's church, a building that dates from the 12th century, and largely rebuilt in the 15th century. Prestbury Park, home to the famous National Hunt Gold Cup meeting each March, is nearby.

WINCHCOMBE, *The George Inn c1960* W378020

Winchcombe's main street has changed remarkably little in the past four decades. It remains a thriving thoroughfare of small shops that cater for the locals' needs to this day. On the right of the picture, behind the railings, are the town's stocks. Last used in 1860, they have seven leg holes, which is curious.

WINCHCOMBE
Abbey Terrace c1955
W378011

A Benedictine abbey stood just off the town square, a vast church that dated from Saxon days. At the time of Dissolution of the Monasteries, Henry VIII gave the people of Winchcombe the opportunity to buy the building. They declined, and instead used the abbey as a source of building materials.

WINCHCOMBE, *Hailes Street c1960* W378021

Like many other Cotswold towns, Winchcombe's fortunes rested on the wool trade. But in Charles II's time, fortunes were also made locally by growing tobacco. When the crop was banned, local farmers refused to give up its cultivation. Samuel Pepys noted in his diary: 'The Life Guard was sent down into the country to Winchcome to spoil the tobacco there which it seems the people there do plant contrary to the law'. Enraged locals sent the king's crack troops packing.

▼ **WINCHCOMBE,** *A Half-Timbered House, Hailes Street c1955* W378009

Wool workers' cottages of this kind traditionally had stable-style front doors. The top half was left open so that merchants could look in and inspect the quality of the work.

► **WINCHCOMBE**
Gloucester Street 1907
59459

Looking down Gloucester Street, this view shows St Peter's in the distance. This 15th-century church is noted for its grotesque gargoyles. The interior was substantially renovated in 1872. To the right in the middle distance is a covered handcart, a typical delivery vehicle of its time.

◀ **STROUD**
*From Rodborough
1900* 45729

Abundant, fast-flowing streams made Stroud an important mill town in the Middle Ages, when water wheels turned the stones that ground the corn. By the 16th century the town was closely connected with the cloth trade, and became famous for the scarlet woollen fabric from which the uniforms of British soldiers were made.

▶ **STROUD**
King Street 1900
45733

In the right foreground is the entrance to Lewis & Godfrey, a local drapers and department store that specialised in 'Admiralty serges'. When this photograph was taken, the four-story building facing the camera with three gabled windows in the roof was The Royal George Hotel, which looked onto King Street Parade. It closed as a hotel within a few years, and was converted for retail use.

STROUD
King Street 1910 62679

A pair of ladies in fashionable Edwardian costume stroll along the raised pavement of Rowcroft on their way to the shops of King Street. A little ahead of them is a gas lamp standard. Horse-drawn transport was not without its pollution problems, evidence of which can be seen littering the surface of the street.

STROUD
Cains Cross 1925 77567

The DD registration tells us that the car chugging its way into town from the direction of Nailsworth was local, registered in Gloucestershire. A number of car and motor cycle makers had factories in Stroud at this time. The largest manufacturer was Hampton Cars, which was based at Dudbridge on the site now occupied by Sainsbury's.

► **STROUD**
*Butter Row,
Old Pyke House
1925* 77568

In days gone by there was a gate across the road at this point which barred the way to passers-by, who could only proceed on payment of a toll. These payments were collected at the toll, or pyke, house, the octagonal, Gothic-style building pictured here. Above the doorway is the list of 'Tolls authorised to be taken at this gate. For any drove of oxen, cows...one halfpenny.'

◄ **STROUD**
George Street c1955
S224024

By the mid 1950s, post-war rationing was coming to an end, and local shops were once again offering a choice of goods. Cars were taking to the roads once more, as petrol became more freely available with the reintroduction of branded fuel in February 1953.

▲ **STROUD,** *On the Canal 1900* 45738

The Stroudwater Canal was built between 1775 and 1779. Its purpose was to allow easier transportation of cloth and manufactured goods from Stroud, while also enabling food and fuel to be brought into the heavily populated area. By the time this photograph was taken, railways had superseded canals, leaving this once thriving lifeline a peaceful backwater.

◀**STOW-ON-THE-WOLD** *The Square c1965* S260050

The King's Arms (left) is a fine example of a coaching inn and former posting house. Stables to the rear were reached through the archway leading from the town square. It is possible that the inn was licensed by Edward VI in 1548. Another royal connection is that Charles I is said to have stayed here at the time of the Battle of Naseby.

STOW-ON-THE-WOLD
The Cross c1955
S260038

Stow's ancient cross in the Square served as a reminder to market traders in medieval times that they should not try to pull the wool over their customers' eyes. A plaque on the cross commemorates Joseph Chamberlayn, who gave £2,000 to install a fresh water supply to the town.

STOW-ON-THE-WOLD, *The Square c1955* S260037

Squeezed between buildings in the Square are alleys, known locally as tures. These follow the patterns of old burgage strips, and on market days, sheep were driven in single file along the narrow ways to be counted.

STOW-ON-THE-WOLD
The Square and the Church c1950 S260022

The building of the parish church of St Edward was funded by wealthy Cotswold wool merchants. Above the north aisle is a Pre-Raphaelite stained glass window designed by Sidney Meteyard and made in 1921 by H H Martyn & Company, the Cheltenham firm of artist-craftsmen.

STOW-ON-THE-WOLD, *The Unicorn Hotel, Sheep Street c1950* S260012

Sheep Street is an appropriate reminder that this town, which sits on a rounded tump 800 feet above sea level, was once a centre of the wool industry. Sheep known as Cotswold Lions were best suited to the conditions, a hardy breed with fleeces especially thick to keep out the chill and make their owners rich.

SLAD
The Valley 1910 62705

The village of Slad sits in one of the loveliest valleys in Gloucestershire. Its most famous son was the author and poet Laurie Lee, who was born in Stroud in 1914 and moved to Slad when he was three, and recalled his childhood in *Cider With Rosie*. At the age of 19 Lee walked to London, then on to civil war-stricken Spain. His memories are captured in *As I Walked Out One Midsummer Morning*.

▼ **SLAD,** *The Village 1910* 62706

Slad huddles round the road that runs from Stroud to Birdlip. When this photograph was taken, the village was an isolated rural community with most of its inhabitants engaged in agriculture. Then as now, an important meeting place for local people was The Woolpack Inn.

▶ **BURFORD**
High Street c1965
B369018

This picturesque Cotswold town in Oxfordshire lies on the slope of a steep hill above the Windrush valley about 20 miles east of Cheltenham. In the broad High Street old inns, houses, small shops and buildings in honey-coloured local stone jostle in a medley of complementary styles. Beyond the war memorial in this view we glimpse the spire of the church of St John the Baptist, where during the Civil War some 340 troops from the Parliamentarian army were held prisoner.

◄ BURFORD
High Street c1955
B369007

Here in the right foreground we see the Tolsey building raised on columns, with its broad clock projecting from the gable. In past times, the Tolsey was the centre of local administration, and taxes were paid here. Adding to the charm of this peaceful scene is the avenue of pollarded limes on the verges higher up the hill.

► BURFORD
The Bridge Approach c1965
B369014

Like many other Cotswold towns, Burford's fortunes were founded on wool, but leather and paper making were also important industries. Rich merchants and tradesfolk built houses for themselves along the town's streets, which is why grand dwellings and humble cottages can be seen cheek by jowl. It was after a visit to Burford in 1876 that William Morris was so appalled by restoration work underway in the church that he drafted the letter which led to the formation of the Society for the Protection of Ancient Buildings.

ASCOTT-UNDER-WYCHWOOD
The Village c1950
A140009

Wychwood is an ancient deciduous forest in the North Cotswolds, and a string of picturesque villages take their names from it: Milton-under-Wychwood, Shipton-under-Wychwood and, glimpsed here as it was half a century ago, Ascott-under-Wychwood.

ASCOTT-UNDER-WYCHWOOD, *The Green c1950* A140003

Tom, Dick and Harry - three brothers with the surname Dunston, who were notorious highwaymen - plied their trade in Wychwood Forest in the latter half of the 18th century. The trio rose to infamy by holding up the Gloucester to Oxford stage coach. But their attempt to burgle Tangley Manor between Stow and Burford went less well. The household had been tipped off, and laid a trap. When Dick put his arm through the grille in the front door to unlatch the lock, his arm was noosed and held fast. Rather than let him be caught, Dick's brothers lopped his arm off.

ASCOTT-UNDER-WYCHWOOD
Church View c1950
A140007

Like other villages that are found along the course of the River Evenlode and its tributary streams, Ascott-under-Wychwood's function was milling. Settlements grew up around the mills powered by fast-running streams that manufactured woollen cloth and ground corn.

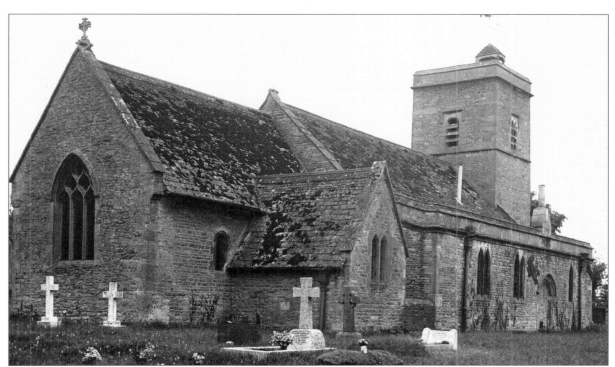

ASCOTT-UNDER-WYCHWOOD, *The Church c1950* A140004

As the population of this essentially agricultural area grew, numerous Cotswold churches expanded from their tiny, Norman origins to accommodate the increasing congregation. The work was often funded by wealthy local merchants, particularly those in the wool trade. Piecemeal expansion is evident in many churches in the region, as is it here.

BIBURY, *Arlington Row c1960* B530023

One of the most picturesque - and most photographed - groups of cottages in the Cotswolds, Arlington Row's first function was as a barn. Then in the 17th century the building was converted into home workers' cottages for weavers in the wool trade. Arlington Row is now owned by the National Trust.

BIBURY, *Saxon Stone in the North Side of the Church Wall c1960* B530010

At first glimpse Bibury church, with its castellated roofline and square tower, looks largely 15th-century. On closer examination, however, the fabric's earlier origins become evident. Set into the north, or 'Devil's side' of the building, is this Saxon motif of interlocking rings, a reminder that the town was once part of the ancient kingdom of Mercia.

BIBURY
The Mill c1960 B530006

The River Coln played an essential role in Bibury's development. From Saxon times it provided the motive power for local corn and cloth mills, in addition to feeding the local system of water meadows, which were made fertile by regular flooding. Bibury is a well-spread-out settlement. This is because it was formed from a number of tiny hamlets and individual properties that gradually grew together over the centuries.

71

BIBURY, *Arlington Manor c1960* B530028

The manor is mentioned in the Domesday book, the detailed survey of property which was conceived by William the Conqueror at Christmas 1085 in Gloucester. We know from this record that a mill stood on the site now occupied by Arlington Mill Museum with its milling machinery and country bygones, although the present building is substantially 17th-century.

BIBURY, *The Swan Hotel c1960* B530027

A popular venue to this day, The Swan Hotel has been providing accommodation and refreshment to guests for over 200 years. William Morris called Bibury the most beautiful village in England. Many of the thousands of visitors who arrive each year drawn by the trout farm and other local attractions probably leave in agreement with him.

BIBURY
The Bibury Court Hotel c1960 B530017

Dating from the 16th century, this fine Tudor country house was planned around three sides of a quadrangle with a protruding porch at the entrance. In plan this shape forms the letter E to celebrate Queen Elizabeth I, who ruled England from 1533 to 1603. Other grand houses in the Cotswolds, such as Chastleton House near Moreton-in-the-Marsh, are built in a similar design.

CHARLBURY, *Sheep Street c1950* C444008

What a peaceful scene is captured here on camera. It is early morning in Charlbury, an Oxfordshire village on the River Evenlode. The proprietor of J L Brooks' ironmongery shop has not yet opened the shop's wrought iron entrance gate. Albert Bowen, licensee of the Hunt, Edmunds & Co pub is not yet serving Banbury ales, wines and spirits. But for the young girl with the satchel on her back, the start of another school day beckons.

CHALFORD
General View 1900
45588A

The Thames and Severn canal opened in 1789, connecting the River Severn with the Thames at Lechlade. It provided the corn and cloth mills of Chalford with the means of finding new markets for their wares until this mode of transport was superseded by the Gloucester to Swindon railway line. The canal closed to commercial trade in 1933.

CHALFORD, *The Hill c1960* C569011

Chalford always was - and remains - a curious blend of the picturesque and industrial. Houses with terraced gardens climb the steep sided Golden Valley and overlook some of the most lovely scenery in the region. Below them meanders the River Frome, with canal and railway line running in parallel, flanked by foundries and business parks.

CHIPPING CAMPDEN
The Almshouses and the Church c1960
C335394

'Chipping' means 'market' in Old English, and it was as a market centre for the woollen industry that Chipping Campden rose to affluence. The town boasts many fine stone buildings, including the early 17th-century almshouses we can see in the foreground here and St James' church - one of the most magnificent in the Cotswolds - beyond.

CHIPPING CAMPDEN, *High Street c1955* C335026

Presiding over the town's broad High Street is the 120 feet high, pinnacle-topped tower of St James', which dates from the 15th century. In the churchyard a tombstone to Martha Hiron, who died in 1708, bears this verse: 'Here lieth a virgin pure and chaste, Who did not want her time to waste. She dearly longed to married be, To Christ her Lord and none but he. And now she has her soul at rest, With glorious sounds for ever blest.'

CHIPPING CAMPDEN
The Market Hall c1955
C335019

The arched building in the left foreground is the Market Hall, which was built in 1627 at the expense of Sir Baptist Hicks. This rich London merchant won favour with James I by lending the monarch money. In return the king granted Hicks 'our rectory and church at Cheltenham, our chapel at Charlton Kings and our church at Campden.' This made Hicks a powerful landowner in the area, and to proclaim the fact he built himself an impressive seat named Campden House. During the Civil War, he burnt the house down for fear that it might fall into Parliamentarian hands.

CHIPPING CAMPDEN, *High Street c1955* C335031

Only the Austin 8 and the cars parked behind it suggest that the camera clicked on this scene half a century ago. Chipping Campden has changed little hereabouts - in fact you can pop into The Volunteer for a pint to this day. Perhaps the author Graham Greene did just that. He lived in the town in the 1930s, working on his novels *Rumours at Nightfall* and *Stamboul Train*.

CHIPPING CAMPDEN
High Street c1955
C335014

In 1902 the architect Charles Ashbee brought 100 silversmiths, furniture makers and other craftsmen with their families from London's East End to establish the Guild of Handicraft in Chipping Campden. Inspired by the Arts and Crafts movement, they set up business in a former silk mill in Sheep Street. To this day the town remains a centre of fine craftsmanship.

TETBURY, *The View from Cutwell c1955* T155034

This Cotswold market town possesses one of the greatest concentrations of protected buildings in the country. Among them is the parish church of St Mary the Virgin. In 1777 the medieval church was demolished and replaced by the Gothic Revival building designed by Francis Hiorn of Worcester we see today. Its spire is the fourth highest in England.

TETBURY, *The Market House c1955* T155043

Tetbury's Town Hall, or Market House, is one of the grandest of its kind found in the Cotswolds, and for centuries has been at the hub of the town's life and business. Built in 1655, it was enlarged in 1740 to accommodate Tetbury's fire engine and lock-up. On the stone roof, topping the decorative cupola, is a weather vane that features a pair of dolphins. Legend relates that the lord of the manor of Tetbury was sailing across the Irish Sea when his ship was holed and began to sink. After praying that he might be saved, two dolphins appeared and wedged themselves in the hole, thus saving the lord's life.

► **TETBURY**
Long Street 1949
T155019

Tetbury's history dates to pre-Roman times, though the first written record appears in AD 681 in reference to a Saxon monastery. During the Middle Ages, the town's prosperity grew with the woollen industry, and it became an important yarn market. Tetbury was largely undisturbed by the Industrial Revolution, which is why this Cotswold gem retains so many ancient buildings of timeless charm.

◄ **TETBURY**
Long Street c1960
T155045

Long Street, which was once known as West Street, has been the main artery of Tetbury since at least the 16th century. There are some fine buildings here, many of them ancient, but one or two are deceptive - The Ormond's Head, for example. Originally an Elizabethan building, this was knocked down in late Victorian times and rebuilt as a mock coaching inn.

▲ **TETBURY,** *Long Street Corner c1955* T155023

On Ash Wednesday and St Mary Magdalene's Day (22 July) each year, a fun fair is staged in the Chipping. 'Chipping' is the Anglo-Saxon word for 'market', and the fairs were once 'mops', at which farm and domestic servants sold their labour to an employer for the year ahead. The fine half-timbered corner premises that in the 1950s housed Fawkes Stores is now a clothes shop. On the opposite side of the road is The Snooty Fox, once called The White Hart, which in the mid 19th century was enlarged to include assembly rooms, where fashionable balls were held.

◀ **TETBURY**
The Green c1965 T155074

Once the centre of the Anglo-Saxon village, the Green is overlooked by houses mostly dating from the 16th and 17th centuries. The exceptions are the Roman Catholic church of St Michael, which was built in 1871 as a Primitive Baptist chapel, and Barton Abbotts, an impressive mid 18th-century house built by the wool stapler William Savage. The popular Victorian novelist George John Whyte-Melville lived here until he was killed in a hunting accident.

TETBURY, *Chipping Steps c1965* T155080

This picturesque quarter of Tetbury leads from the north-east corner of the Chipping to a triangular green with a splendid copper beech tree. Nearby, Chipping Croft is a 17th-century house to which an elegant balcony was added in Regency times.

TETBURY
*Westonbirt School
c1955* T155021

Besides its famous school, Westonbirt is best known for its arboretum, which boasts one of the largest collections of trees and shrubs in the world. The 600-acre site is owned by the Forestry Commission, and offers 17 miles of paths to explore. Among the 18,000 specimens are over 100 'champion' trees - the oldest, tallest and so on. Beautiful all year round, Westonbirt is especially magical in the autumn.

CHIPPING NORTON, *The King Stone, the Rollright Stones c1960* C288070

Not far from Chipping Norton, close to Long Compton, stands a Bronze Age circle of 77 stones, a group of Neolithic upright stones and the single, 8 feet tall King Stone shown here, which dates from the Bronze Age. According to local lore, a king in ancient times set out to conquer England and was met at this spot by a witch, who pronounced: 'Seven long strides shalt thou take, if Long Compton thou can see, then king of England thou shalt be. If Long Compton thou cannot see, then king of England thou shalt not be.' For a reason that the legend does not make clear, the witch then turned the would-be monarch and his followers into stones.

▼ **CHIPPING NORTON,** *The Cotswolds c1960* C288067

The Cotswold uplands average 700 feet above sea level, but in places rise to over just over 1,000 feet. Most of the region's towns have fine buildings and churches paid for by the wool trade that flourished in these parts. It is said that the name Cotswold originated because of the cotes (sheep pens) that were found across the wolds (rolling hills). When the woollen industry went into decline, arable crops replaced the sheep, giving rise to the gentle, predominantly agricultural landscape we see here.

► **CHIPPING NORTON**
Market Place c1955
C288028

The large open Market Square hints at the importance of this Oxfordshire town as a trading place for the surrounding population in the past. A prominent feature seen here is the Town Hall, ingeniously constructed on land that is far from level in the 19th century. The coach seen in this photograph tells us that even by the 1950s Chipping Norton's attraction had placed it firmly on the tourist trail.

◄ **CHIPPING NORTON**
Market Street c1945
C288009

What a wonderful mish-mash of buildings are captured on camera here. Some are grand, others less so, but regardless of size or style they blend perfectly because they are made from the same rosy-hued local stone. Just outside the town stands Bliss Tweed Mills, built by George Woodhouse in 1872, whose thriving clothing business provided 700 jobs. The mill, topped by a soaring chimney stack, closed in 1981 and has since been converted into housing.

► **CHIPPING NORTON**
Market Street c1960 C288045

A little out of shot is the church of St Mary, which has an unusual gravestone in memory of Phillis Humphreys, who died at the age of 58 in 1763. The inscription described her as a 'rat catcher who has lodged in many a town and travelled far and near. By age and death she is struck down to her last lodging here.'

CHIPPING NORTON
The Crown and Cushion Hotel c1960
C288058

As the highest town in Oxfordshire, Chipping Norton must have been reached only after a struggle in the days of horse-drawn travel. The town was an important stopping-off point on the coaching route between Worcester and London, and consequently it is well-served with fine old country pubs and inns with courtyards that once rang to the clatter of hooves and iron-rimmed wheels on cobble stones.

CHIPPING NORTON, *New Street c1960* C288066

An element of the town's charm is that it is built on different levels, which are joined by narrow lanes and flights of steps. There has been a settlement on this spot since Saxon times, but the present town was developed in the 13th century by the lord of the manor to take advantage of its position at the convergence of important travel and trade routes

LECHLADE
The Round House
c1960 L147026

Although it looks like a Gothic folly, this roundhouse was lived in by a lengthmen and his family who collected tolls from passing barges on the Thames and Severn canal. Built in the latter half of the 18th century, this man-made waterway stretched from Inglesham to Stroud, where it joined the Stroudwater Navigation leading to the River Severn at Framilode.

LECHLADE, *The River c1955* L147045

The toll house on the far span of Halfpenny Bridge explains the unusual name, because that is how much it cost to pass over this handsome construction when it was built in the 18th century. The road that crosses the bridge leading out of Lechlade brings the traveller to Inglesham, which has a Saxon church that was much admired by William Morris.

▼ **LECHLADE,** *Church Street c1955* L147013

St Lawrence's church was built in the Perpendicular style and paid for by merchants made rich from wool. Grotesque gargoyles (like those at Winchcombe church) look down from the church into the Market Square. Some of the town's fine Georgian buildings can be seen here.

► **LECHLADE**
Oak Street c1955 L147012

Lechlade was once a market town, but was overshadowed in this function by its near neighbour Fairford. Nevertheless, Lechlade played host to a livestock fair until the late 1950s.

◀ **LECHLADE**
High Street c1955
L147008

The wide arched entrance to The New Inn is a reminder that Lechlade was once an important coaching town. Stage coaches brought people and business to the town, and in years gone by the streets rang to the clatter of hooves as carriages arrived and left. Dotted about the town are curious small, square gazebos. These were the bus shelters of their time, in which travellers took refuge from the weather while awaiting their carriages.

▶ **LECHLADE**
St John's Lock c1960
L147304

This is the highest lock on the River Thames, which was at one time an important artery of commerce and trade. By the time this photograph was taken, though, only pleasure craft plied these waters. In the distance, across the water meadows, the spire-topped tower of St Lawrence's church beckons.

LECHLADE
The Moorings c1955
L147006

In the 17th century, Lechlade was the venue for one of the largest cheese fairs in the south-west. Wharves and warehouses were built alongside the river to accommodate the trade in cheeses from all parts of Gloucestershire and North Wiltshire. Until the railways came, coal from the Forest of Dean also arrived on board barges.

LECHLADE
*The Mill and the
Lock Gates c1955*
L147037

Water and water power
have had a strong
influence on the
development of the
town, which is hardly
surprising, as it stands at
the confluence of three
rivers, the Thames, the
Coln and the Leach.

LECHLADE, *The Convent of St Clotilde c1960* L147039

Lechlade Manor was built by George Milward. The architect John Pearson completed the designs in 1872, and the shell was
erected for a modest £8,850. George Milward went bankrupt in 1886, and after changing hands a number of times, Lechlade
Manor was sold to the nuns of St Clotilde in 1939. The house remained a girls' boarding school until 1997.

LECHLADE
The Trout Inn
c1955 L147016

The poet Percy Bysshe Shelley rowed to Lechlade from Windsor with his friends Mary Godwin, Thomas Love Peacock and Charles Clairmont in 1815. The visit inspired him to write *Stanzas in a Summer Evening Churchyard*. As this photograph reminds us, by the mid 1950s private cars and public buses opened the pleasures of Lechlade to a wider audience.

DURSLEY, *General View 1904* 51949

As well as the tower of St James' church, a number of industrial chimney stacks punctuate the town skyline, hinting at Dursley's manufacturing past. Besides cloth making, the town became a centre for the manufacture of agricultural machinery; this was thanks to Robert Ashton Lister, who set up his firm in 1845. His son Percy expanded the business, and began production of the diesel engines that are made to this day. In the 1890s, Lister's chief engineer was a Danish man, Mikael Pedersen, who invented a safety bicycle and the milk churn.

FAIRFORD
The Bridge c1955 F145026

The River Coln flows through Fairford on its way to meet the Thames just a few meandering miles on. The town has its place in the history of aviation, for on 9 April 1969 Captain Brian Trubshaw flew Concorde 002 from Filton in Bristol to RAF Fairford, which was the aircraft's flight test base for the next seven years.

► **FAIRFORD**
The Mill and Bridge
c1950 F145007

Beyond the mill, which dates from Norman times, is the square tower of St Mary's. This parish church has some fine stained glass in 28 windows paid for by John Tame, a rich wool merchant. According to local legend, the glass was captured by John Tame as it was on its way to Rome by ship. The truth is more likely to be that the windows arrived in this country by ship from Flanders, where many of them were made.

◄ **FAIRFORD**
High Street c1955
F145023

Like other wool towns in the Cotswolds, such as Stroud, Painswick and Woodchester, Fairford has a 'Rack Hill'. This name recalls the place where cloth was stretched out to dry after dyeing or fulling. John Keble, writer of *The Christian Year* and a leading light in the Oxford Movement, was born in Fairford in 1792, and the American artist Edwin Austin Abbey came to live in the town in 1878.

▲ **FAIRFORD,** *London Street 1948* F145010

In the days of horse-drawn travel, Fairford was an important coaching town that straddled the important road leading to the capital from the south-west. Local inns thrived on the trade, providing food, drink and accommodation for travellers, plus fresh horses for the stagecoach companies.

◄ **NAILSWORTH**
The Cross c1965 N1057

This view looks down towards the Cross from the A46 Bath Road. At the bottom of the slope is the clock tower and George Street, in which is found one of the largest kettles in the country. It hangs some five metres above street level and has been there for about 80 years, originally as an advertisement for the Copper Kettle Tea Shop. Said to hold 80 gallons, the kettle is reckoned to weigh over one hundredweight.

NAILSWORTH
Fountain Street c1965
N1055

Behind the tree on the left is the church of St George, built during the reign of Queen Victoria. It is also worth noting that all the cars seen here in Fountain Street - an Austin A40, a P4 Rover, a Morris 1000 Traveller, an Austin 1100, two Minis and a Ford Anglia approaching - are British-built. What a rare sight that would be today.

NAILSWORTH
General View 1900 45595

The stone cottages built for mill workers look picturesque, but in days gone by conditions were by no means luxurious. It is recorded that in the 1920s such cottages, with their flagstone floors laid directly on the earth and exterior walls with no dampcourse, were difficult to keep warm and dry. To try and improve their comfort, residents laid linoleum over the flagstones to stop the damp rising. Next coconut matting was placed over the linoleum, which in turn was covered with home made rugs stitched together from strips of cloth.

MINCHINHAMPTON, *The Church c1960* M83064

The most striking feature of Holy Trinity church is its truncated spire, which was snipped in 1563 for fear of collapse. Situated high up on the eastern edge of the 580-acre Minchinhampton Common, now in the care of the National Trust, this attractive old cloth town is rich in the variety and architectural style of its buildings.

MINCHINHAMPTON, *The Church, the Rose Window 1901* 47353

Holy Trinity overlooks the north end of the High Street, although it stands a little apart as though distancing itself from temporal affairs. Besides this magnificent rose window, the church has a splendid 14th-century south transept, intricate vaulting beneath the tower, and some interesting brasses, including a pair of shrouded corpses.

MINCHINHAMPTON
Market Square c1955
M83055

The town's fine Market House dates from 1698; it rests on an arcade of pillars that are unusual in that they are made of stone on the outside, and timber on the inside. Another feature of the Market Square is the Crown Hotel, built in the 18th century. Market houses of this design are found throughout the Cotswolds. The upper storey often served as the town hall, while market traders set up their stalls beneath.

WOODCHESTER, *The Roman Catholic Church 1890* 25178

William Leigh bought the Woodchester estate in 1845. A wealthy merchant from Liverpool, he had recently converted to the Roman Catholic faith; having donated £4,000 to build a cathedral in Adelaide, he now wanted to establish a monastic community in the Cotswolds. The monastery was built in Woodchester, and part of it - the Church of Our Lady - can be seen in the village to this day. The rest, however, was demolished in 1970.

WOODCHESTER, *The Church 1900* 45593

Built in the Victorian Gothic style, Woodchester church was constructed in the early 1860s. By that time, building work on William Leigh's plan for a grand mansion at nearby Woodchester Park had been under way for six years. Unfortunately, Leigh suffered family tragedy when his two daughters died. His health failed, and in 1873 he died at the age of 70. Consequently his mansion was left unfinished. In 1989 the Woodchester Mansion Trust, a group of volunteers dedicated to the preservation of the building, assumed responsibility. Since then the house has been used as a training centre for stonemasons, and it is opened to the public on certain weekends during the summer months.

WOODCHESTER
General View, 1900
45591

Sitting on a steep slope of the Avon Valley between Stroud and Nailsworth, Woodchester is home to one of the best Roman mosaic pavements in the country. It was discovered when the remains of a large Roman villa were excavated in 1796.

WOODCHESTER, *The Amberley Inn c1960* W130504

This Cotswold stone hostelry takes its name from the nearby village of Amberley, which boasts a number of literary associations. Dinah Mulock lived here in Rose Cottage, and won considerable success with her novel *John Halifax, Gentleman* when it was published in 1857 under her pseudonym of Mrs Craik. The popular Victorian poet Sydney Thompson Dobell visited the village in 1853, and the author of *Beau Geste*, P C Wren, is buried in the churchyard.

SOUTH CERNEY
The Village c1965
S517007

It is easy to understand why this quarter of South Cerney, with its squat stone cottages ranged along the banks of the River Churn, are often photographed by day trippers. Less simple to fathom are some of the village street names. The lane in the centre of the village that crosses the bridge is called 'Bow Wow', while not far off is another named 'Upper Up'.

SOUTH CERNEY, *The Manor, the Park and the Church c1965* S517001

At the entrance to the Norman church is a notice that reads: *'Enter this door as if the floor within were gold/ And every wall of jewels, of wealth untold./ As if a choir/ In robes of fire/ Were saying here/ Nor shout, not rush/ But hush/ For God is here.'* Another curiosity is found close by on the road to Cirencester, where a stone building in the shape of a chess rook can be seen. This folly was built by a Dutchman in the 18th century. Why? Nobody knows.

▼ **SOUTH CERNEY,** *The Water Park c1965* S517010

There are over 130 lakes in the Water Park, making it the largest man-made complex of its kind in Britain. The lakes are the result of rich sand and gravel deposits that have been extracted from this area for the past half century.

▶ **SOUTH CERNEY**
The Memorial c1965
S517012

Beyond the war memorial is a drystone wall topped by the sign that reads Broadway Lane. A typical feature of the Cotswolds, the centuries old craft of drystone walling flourishes to the present day.

◄ **LOWER SLAUGHTER**
The Mill c1960
L313004

The River Eye flows through the village on its way to join the River Dickler, which in turn feeds the Windrush to the south of Bourton-on-the-Water. The plentiful supply of streams and rivers provided water power for corn and cloth mills all over the Cotswolds. There has been a mill on this site at Lower Slaughter since before the Norman conquest, though the building shown here dates from around 1800.

► **LOWER SLAUGHTER**
The Village c1960 L313011

It is difficult to imagine a more peaceful scene, but during the Second World War things were not always so tranquil. The high plateau of the Cotswolds was home to many airfields brought into service during the conflict. In 1939 an RAF bomber en route for the airfield at nearby Windrush from Andover narrowly missed Lower Slaughter and crash-landed near Upper Slaughter in a field 50 yards from the church.

LOWER SLAUGHTER
The Stream c1955
L313002

The names of Lower Slaughter and its near namesake Upper Slaughter may suggest a bloodthirsty episode in the history of their surroundings. The truth, however, is far less fearsome. Some old guide books claim the name derives from the sloe (or blackthorn) tree, but it more likely comes from 'slough', meaning a muddy place.

▼ **CRANHAM,** *The Old House c1965* C179058

Notice how the limestone roof slates are smaller at the ridge, becoming larger as they descend towards the eaves of this fine old house. This is typical of a Cotswold roof, which has to be steeply pitched because the slates are porous, so water must run off quickly. The original part of the house was built in 1687, but there are later additions.

▶ **CRANHAM**
The Woods 1907 59069

This large area of deciduous woods, in which beech predominates, is a favourite with walkers. Prinknash Abbey stands on the lower slopes, a small Benedictine community that moved here from Caldey Island in 1928. The original abbey was here in the 14th century, but a 20th-century monastic building is in use today. Another community - the Scouts Association - also has an HQ in Cranham Woods.

◀ CRANHAM
The Village c1960
C179007

In days gone by, the lake at Cranham was the local swimming pool for children in such neighbouring villages as Sheepscombe, Birdlip and Brimpsfield. Those of riper years were drawn to the village pub, The Black Horse, reached like a reward after climbing the steep rise on which it stands.

▶ ULEY
The Tumulus c1960 U3008

This Neolithic long barrow was built around 2,500 BC, and the remains of 28 human skeletons were found when the site was excavated in 1854. A mile north of Uley there is another long barrow, known as Hetty Pegler's Tump. The story goes that in the 17th century the land on which this ancient monument stood belonged to a woman named Hetty Pegler, who enjoyed nothing more than to sit on the pagan grave and sing.

ULEY
The Street c1960 U3020

Good examples of 18th-century architecture can be seen in Uley; one is The King's Head, with a brightly painted sign outside that dates from the time of George I. The village rose to prosperity as a cloth making centre, but when the Industrial Revolution shifted production from weavers' cottages to industrial factories, Uley's fortunes went into decline.

113

ULEY, *The Village c1960* U3004

This picture captures reminders of road transport old and new. In the foreground is a toll house, a vestige from the days of horse-drawn coaches that paid to use the road. Approaching from the middle distance is a single-decker motor bus. Today, of course, most of the wheels that roll this way belong to private cars.

INDEX

Frith Book Co Titles

www.francisfrith.co.uk

The Frith Book Company publishes over 100 new titles each year. A selection of those currently available is listed below. For latest catalogue please contact Frith Book Co.
Town Books 96 pages, approximately 100 photos. **County and Themed Books** 128 pages, approximately 150 photos (unless specified). All titles hardback with laminated case and jacket, except those indicated pb (paperback)

Amersham, Chesham & Rickmansworth (pb)	1-85937-340-2	£9.99	Devon (pb)	1-85937-297-x	£9.99
Andover (pb)	1-85937-292-9	£9.99	Devon Churches (pb)	1-85937-250-3	£9.99
Aylesbury (pb)	1-85937-227-9	£9.99	Dorchester (pb)	1-85937-307-0	£9.99
Barnstaple (pb)	1-85937-300-3	£9.99	Dorset (pb)	1-85937-269-4	£9.99
Basildon Living Memories (pb)	1-85937-515-4	£9.99	Dorset Coast (pb)	1-85937-299-6	£9.99
Bath (pb)	1-85937-419-0	£9.99	Dorset Living Memories (pb)	1-85937-584-7	£9.99
Bedford (pb)	1-85937-205-8	£9.99	Down the Severn (pb)	1-85937-560-x	£9.99
Bedfordshire Living Memories	1-85937-513-8	£14.99	Down The Thames (pb)	1-85937-278-3	£9.99
Belfast (pb)	1-85937-303-8	£9.99	Down the Trent	1-85937-311-9	£14.99
Berkshire (pb)	1-85937-191-4	£9.99	East Anglia (pb)	1-85937-265-1	£9.99
Berkshire Churches	1-85937-170-1	£17.99	East Grinstead (pb)	1-85937-138-8	£9.99
Berkshire Living Memories	1-85937-332-1	£14.99	East London	1-85937-080-2	£14.99
Black Country	1-85937-497-2	£12.99	East Sussex (pb)	1-85937-606-1	£9.99
Blackpool (pb)	1-85937-393-3	£9.99	Eastbourne (pb)	1-85937-399-2	£9.99
Bognor Regis (pb)	1-85937-431-x	£9.99	Edinburgh (pb)	1-85937-193-0	£8.99
Bournemouth (pb)	1-85937-545-6	£9.99	England In The 1880s	1-85937-331-3	£17.99
Bradford (pb)	1-85937-204-x	£9.99	Essex - Second Selection	1-85937-456-5	£14.99
Bridgend (pb)	1-85937-386-0	£7.99	Essex (pb)	1-85937-270-8	£9.99
Bridgwater (pb)	1-85937-305-4	£9.99	Essex Coast	1-85937-342-9	£14.99
Bridport (pb)	1-85937-327-5	£9.99	Essex Living Memories	1-85937-490-5	£14.99
Brighton (pb)	1-85937-192-2	£8.99	Exeter	1-85937-539-1	£9.99
Bristol (pb)	1-85937-264-3	£9.99	Exmoor (pb)	1-85937-608-8	£9.99
British Life A Century Ago (pb)	1-85937-213-9	£9.99	Falmouth (pb)	1-85937-594-4	£9.99
Buckinghamshire (pb)	1-85937-200-7	£9.99	Folkestone (pb)	1-85937-124-8	£9.99
Camberley (pb)	1-85937-222-8	£9.99	Frome (pb)	1-85937-317-8	£9.99
Cambridge (pb)	1-85937-422-0	£9.99	Glamorgan	1-85937-488-3	£14.99
Cambridgeshire (pb)	1-85937-420-4	£9.99	Glasgow (pb)	1-85937-190-6	£9.99
Cambridgeshire Villages	1-85937-523-5	£14.99	Glastonbury (pb)	1-85937-338-0	£7.99
Canals And Waterways (pb)	1-85937-291-0	£9.99	Gloucester (pb)	1-85937-232-5	£9.99
Canterbury Cathedral (pb)	1-85937-179-5	£9.99	Gloucestershire (pb)	1-85937-561-8	£9.99
Cardiff (pb)	1-85937-093-4	£9.99	Great Yarmouth (pb)	1-85937-426-3	£9.99
Carmarthenshire (pb)	1-85937-604-5	£9.99	Greater Manchester (pb)	1-85937-266-x	£9.99
Chelmsford (pb)	1-85937-310-0	£9.99	Guildford (pb)	1-85937-410-7	£9.99
Cheltenham (pb)	1-85937-095-0	£9.99	Hampshire (pb)	1-85937-279-1	£9.99
Cheshire (pb)	1-85937-271-6	£9.99	Harrogate (pb)	1-85937-423-9	£9.99
Chester (pb)	1-85937-382 8	£9.99	Hastings and Bexhill (pb)	1-85937-131-0	£9.99
Chesterfield (pb)	1-85937-378-x	£9.99	Heart of Lancashire (pb)	1-85937-197-3	£9.99
Chichester (pb)	1-85937-228-7	£9.99	Helston (pb)	1-85937-214-7	£9.99
Churches of East Cornwall (pb)	1-85937-249-x	£9.99	Hereford (pb)	1-85937-175-2	£9.99
Churches of Hampshire (pb)	1-85937-207-4	£9.99	Herefordshire (pb)	1-85937-567-7	£9.99
Cinque Ports & Two Ancient Towns	1-85937-492-1	£14.99	Herefordshire Living Memories	1-85937-514-6	£14.99
Colchester (pb)	1-85937-188-4	£8.99	Hertfordshire (pb)	1-85937-247-3	£9.99
Cornwall (pb)	1-85937-229-5	£9.99	Horsham (pb)	1-85937-432-8	£9.99
Cornwall Living Memories	1-85937-248-1	£14.99	Humberside (pb)	1-85937-605-3	£9.99
Cotswolds (pb)	1-85937-230-9	£9.99	Hythe, Romney Marsh, Ashford (pb)	1-85937-256-2	£9.99
Cotswolds Living Memories	1-85937-255-4	£14.99	Ipswich (pb)	1-85937-424-7	£9.99
County Durham (pb)	1-85937-398-4	£9.99	Isle of Man (pb)	1-85937-268-6	£9.99
Croydon Living Memories (pb)	1-85937-162-0	£9.99	Isle of Wight (pb)	1-85937-429-8	£9.99
Cumbria (pb)	1-85937-621-5	£9.99	Isle of Wight Living Memories	1-85937-304-6	£14.99
Derby (pb)	1-85937-367-4	£9.99	Kent (pb)	1-85937-189-2	£9.99
Derbyshire (pb)	1-85937-196-5	£9.99	Kent Living Memories(pb)	1-85937-401-8	£9.99
Derbyshire Living Memories	1-85937-330-5	£14.99	Kings Lynn (pb)	1-85937-334-8	£9.99

Available from your local bookshop or from the publisher

Frith Book Co Titles (continued)

Title	ISBN	Price	Title	ISBN	Price
Lake District (pb)	1-85937-275-9	£9.99	Sherborne (pb)	1-85937-301-1	£9.99
Lancashire Living Memories	1-85937-335-6	£14.99	Shrewsbury (pb)	1-85937-325-9	£9.99
Lancaster, Morecambe, Heysham (pb)	1-85937-233-3	£9.99	Shropshire (pb)	1-85937-326-7	£9.99
Leeds (pb)	1-85937-202-3	£9.99	Shropshire Living Memories	1-85937-643-6	£14.99
Leicester (pb)	1-85937-381-x	£9.99	Somerset	1-85937-153-1	£14.99
Leicestershire & Rutland Living Memories	1-85937-500-6	£12.99	South Devon Coast	1-85937-107-8	£14.99
Leicestershire (pb)	1-85937-185-x	£9.99	South Devon Living Memories (pb)	1-85937-609-6	£9.99
Lighthouses	1-85937-257-0	£9.99	South East London (pb)	1-85937-263-5	£9.99
Lincoln (pb)	1-85937-380-1	£9.99	South Somerset	1-85937-318-6	£14.99
Lincolnshire (pb)	1-85937-433-6	£9.99	South Wales	1-85937-519-7	£14.99
Liverpool and Merseyside (pb)	1-85937-234-1	£9.99	Southampton (pb)	1-85937-427-1	£9.99
London (pb)	1-85937-183-3	£9.99	Southend (pb)	1-85937-313-5	£9.99
London Living Memories	1-85937-454-9	£14.99	Southport (pb)	1-85937-425-5	£9.99
Ludlow (pb)	1-85937-176-0	£9.99	St Albans (pb)	1-85937-341-0	£9.99
Luton (pb)	1-85937-235-x	£9.99	St Ives (pb)	1-85937-415-8	£9.99
Maidenhead (pb)	1-85937-339-9	£9.99	Stafford Living Memories (pb)	1-85937-503-0	£9.99
Maidstone (pb)	1-85937-391-7	£9.99	Staffordshire (pb)	1-85937-308-9	£9.99
Manchester (pb)	1-85937-198-1	£9.99	Stourbridge (pb)	1-85937-530-8	£9.99
Marlborough (pb)	1-85937-336-4	£9.99	Stratford upon Avon (pb)	1-85937-388-7	£9.99
Middlesex	1-85937-158-2	£14.99	Suffolk (pb)	1-85937-221-x	£9.99
Monmouthshire	1-85937-532-4	£14.99	Suffolk Coast (pb)	1-85937-610-x	£9.99
New Forest (pb)	1-85937-390-9	£9.99	Surrey (pb)	1-85937-240-6	£9.99
Newark (pb)	1-85937-366-6	£9.99	Surrey Living Memories	1-85937-328-3	£14.99
Newport, Wales (pb)	1-85937-258-9	£9.99	Sussex (pb)	1-85937-184-1	£9.99
Newquay (pb)	1-85937-421-2	£9.99	Sutton (pb)	1-85937-337-2	£9.99
Norfolk (pb)	1-85937-195-7	£9.99	Swansea (pb)	1-85937-167-1	£9.99
Norfolk Broads	1-85937-486-7	£14.99	Taunton (pb)	1-85937-314-3	£9.99
Norfolk Living Memories (pb)	1-85937-402-6	£9.99	Tees Valley & Cleveland (pb)	1-85937-623-1	£9.99
North Buckinghamshire	1-85937-626-6	£14.99	Teignmouth (pb)	1-85937-370-4	£7.99
North Devon Living Memories	1-85937-261-9	£14.99	Thanet (pb)	1-85937-116-7	£9.99
North Hertfordshire	1-85937-547-2	£14.99	Tiverton (pb)	1-85937-178-7	£9.99
North London (pb)	1-85937-403-4	£9.99	Torbay (pb)	1-85937-597-9	£9.99
North Somerset	1-85937-302-x	£14.99	Truro (pb)	1-85937-598-7	£9.99
North Wales (pb)	1-85937-298-8	£9.99	Victorian & Edwardian Dorset	1-85937-254-6	£14.99
North Yorkshire (pb)	1-85937-236-8	£9.99	Victorian & Edwardian Kent (pb)	1-85937-624-X	£9.99
Northamptonshire Living Memories	1-85937-529-4	£14.99	Victorian & Edwardian Maritime Album (pb)	1-85937-622-3	£9.99
Northamptonshire	1-85937-150-7	£14.99	Victorian and Edwardian Sussex (pb)	1-85937-625-8	£9.99
Northumberland Tyne & Wear (pb)	1-85937-281-3	£9.99	Villages of Devon (pb)	1-85937-293-7	£9.99
Northumberland	1-85937-522-7	£14.99	Villages of Kent (pb)	1-85937-294-5	£9.99
Norwich (pb)	1-85937-194-9	£8.99	Villages of Sussex (pb)	1-85937-295-3	£9.99
Nottingham (pb)	1-85937-324-0	£9.99	Warrington (pb)	1-85937-507-3	£9.99
Nottinghamshire (pb)	1-85937-187-6	£9.99	Warwick (pb)	1-85937-518-9	£9.99
Oxford (pb)	1-85937-411-5	£9.99	Warwickshire (pb)	1-85937-203-1	£9.99
Oxfordshire (pb)	1-85937-430-1	£9.99	Welsh Castles (pb)	1-85937-322-4	£9.99
Oxfordshire Living Memories	1-85937-525-1	£14.99	West Midlands (pb)	1-85937-289-9	£9.99
Paignton (pb)	1-85937-374-7	£7.99	West Sussex (pb)	1-85937-607-x	£9.99
Peak District (pb)	1-85937-280-5	£9.99	West Yorkshire (pb)	1-85937-201-5	£9.99
Pembrokeshire	1-85937-262-7	£14.99	Weston Super Mare (pb)	1-85937-306-2	£9.99
Penzance (pb)	1-85937-595-2	£9.99	Weymouth (pb)	1-85937-209-0	£9.99
Peterborough (pb)	1-85937-219-8	£9.99	Wiltshire (pb)	1-85937-277-5	£9.99
Picturesque Harbours	1-85937-208-2	£14.99	Wiltshire Churches (pb)	1-85937-171-x	£9.99
Piers	1-85937-237-6	£17.99	Wiltshire Living Memories (pb)	1-85937-396-8	£9.99
Plymouth (pb)	1-85937-389-5	£9.99	Winchester (pb)	1-85937-428-x	£9.99
Poole & Sandbanks (pb)	1-85937-251-1	£9.99	Windsor (pb)	1-85937-333-x	£9.99
Preston (pb)	1-85937-212-0	£9.99	Wokingham & Bracknell (pb)	1-85937-329-1	£9.99
Reading (pb)	1-85937-238-4	£9.99	Woodbridge (pb)	1-85937-498-0	£9.99
Redhill to Reigate (pb)	1-85937-596-0	£9.99	Worcester (pb)	1-85937-165-5	£9.99
Ringwood (pb)	1-85937-384-4	£7.99	Worcestershire Living Memories	1-85937-489-1	£14.99
Romford (pb)	1-85937-319-4	£9.99	Worcestershire	1-85937-152-3	£14.99
Royal Tunbridge Wells (pb)	1-85937-504-9	£9.99	York (pb)	1-85937-199-x	£9.99
Salisbury (pb)	1-85937-239-2	£9.99	Yorkshire (pb)	1-85937-186-8	£9.99
Scarborough (pb)	1-85937-379-8	£9.99	Yorkshire Coastal Memories	1-85937-506-5	£14.99
Sevenoaks and Tonbridge (pb)	1-85937-392-5	£9.99	Yorkshire Dales	1-85937-502-2	£14.99
Sheffield & South Yorks (pb)	1-85937-267-8	£9.99	Yorkshire Living Memories (pb)	1-85937-397-6	£9.99

See Frith books on the internet at www.francisfrith.co.uk

FRITH PRODUCTS & SERVICES

Francis Frith would doubtless be pleased to know that the pioneering publishing venture he started in 1860 still continues today. Over a hundred and forty years later, The Francis Frith Collection continues in the same innovative tradition and is now one of the foremost publishers of vintage photographs in the world. Some of the current activities include:

Interior Decoration

Today Frith's photographs can be seen framed and as giant wall murals in thousands of pubs, restaurants, hotels, banks, retail stores and other public buildings throughout the country. In every case they enhance the unique local atmosphere of the places they depict and provide reminders of gentler days in an increasingly busy and frenetic world.

Product Promotions

Frith products are used by many major companies to promote the sales of their own products or to reinforce their own history and heritage. Frith promotions have been used by Hovis bread, Courage beers, Scots Porage Oats, Colman's mustard, Cadbury's foods, Mellow Birds coffee, Dunhill pipe tobacco, Guinness, and Bulmer's Cider.

Genealogy and Family History

As the interest in family history and roots grows world-wide, more and more people are turning to Frith's photographs of Great Britain for images of the towns, villages and streets where their ancestors lived; and, of course, photographs of the churches and chapels where their ancestors were christened, married and buried are an essential part of every genealogy tree and family album.

Frith Products

All Frith photographs are available Framed or just as Mounted Prints and Posters (size 23 x 16 inches). These may be ordered from the address below. From time to time other products - Address Books, Calendars, Table Mats, etc - are available.

The Internet

Already fifty thousand Frith photographs can be viewed and purchased on the internet through the Frith websites and a myriad of partner sites.

For more detailed information on Frith companies and products, look at these sites:

www.francisfrith.co.uk
www.francisfrith.com
(for North American visitors)

See the complete list of Frith Books at:

www.francisfrith.co.uk

This web site is regularly updated with the latest list of publications from the Frith Book Company. If you wish to buy books relating to another part of the country that your local bookshop does not stock, you may purchase on-line.

For further information, trade, or author enquiries please contact us at the address below:
The Francis Frith Collection, Frith's Barn, Teffont, Salisbury, Wiltshire, England SP3 5QP.
Tel: +44 (0)1722 716 376 Fax: +44 (0)1722 716 881   Email: sales@francisfrith.co.uk

See Frith books on the internet at www.francisfrith.co.uk

FREE MOUNTED PRINT

Mounted Print
Overall size 14 x 11 inches

Fill in and cut out this voucher and return
it with your remittance for £2.25 (to cover postage and handling). Offer valid for delivery to UK addresses only.

Choose any photograph included in this book.
Your SEPIA print will be A4 in size. It will be mounted in a cream mount with a burgundy rule line (overall size 14 x 11 inches).

**Order additional Mounted Prints
at HALF PRICE (only £7.49 each*)**
If you would like to order more Frith prints from this book, possibly as gifts for friends and family, you can buy them at half price (with no additional postage and handling costs).

Have your Mounted Prints framed
For an extra £14.95 per print* you can have your mounted print(s) framed in an elegant polished wood and gilt moulding, overall size 16 x 13 inches (no additional postage and handling required).

---

* IMPORTANT!

These special prices are only available if you order at the same time as you order your free mounted print. You must use the ORIGINAL VOUCHER on this page (no copies permitted). We can only despatch to one address.

Send completed Voucher form to:
The Francis Frith Collection, Frith's Barn, Teffont, Salisbury, Wiltshire SP3 5QP

CHOOSE ANY IMAGE FROM THIS BOOK

Voucher for *FREE* and Reduced Price *Frith Prints*

Please do not photocopy this voucher. Only the original is valid, so please fill it in, cut it out and return it to us with your order.

Picture ref no	Page no	Qty	Mounted @ £7.49	Framed + £14.95	Total Cost
		1	Free of charge*	£	£
			£7.49	£	£
			£7.49	£	£
			£7.49	£	£
			£7.49	£	£
			£7.49	£	£
Please allow 28 days for delivery			* Post & handling (UK)		£2.25
			Total Order Cost		£

Title of this book . . . .

I enclose a cheque/postal order for £ . . . .
made payable to 'The Francis Frith Collection'

OR please debit my Mastercard / Visa / Switch / Amex card
(credit cards please on all overseas orders), details below

Card Number

Issue No (Switch only)   Valid from (Amex/Switch)

Expires   Signature

Name Mr/Mrs/Ms . . . .
Address . . . .
. . . .
. . . .
. . . . Postcode . . . .
Daytime Tel No . . . .
Email . . . .

Valid to 31/12/05

Would you like to find out more about Francis Frith?

We have recently recruited some entertaining speakers who are happy to visit local groups, clubs and societies to give an illustrated talk documenting Frith's travels and photographs. If you are a member of such a group and are interested in hosting a presentation, we would love to hear from you.

Our speakers bring with them a small selection of our local town and county books, together with sample prints. They are happy to take orders. A small proportion of the order value is donated to the group who have hosted the presentation. The talks are therefore an excellent way of fundraising for small groups and societies.

Can you help us with information about any of the Frith photographs in this book?

We are gradually compiling an historical record for each of the photographs in the Frith archive. It is always fascinating to find out the names of the people shown in the pictures, as well as insights into the shops, buildings and other features depicted.

If you recognize anyone in the photographs in this book, or if you have information not already included in the author's caption, do let us know. We would love to hear from you, and will try to publish it in future books or articles.

Our production team

Frith books are produced by a small dedicated team at offices in the converted Grade II listed 18th-century barn at Teffont near Salisbury, illustrated above. Most have worked with the Frith Collection for many years. All have in common one quality: they have a passion for the Frith Collection. The team is constantly expanding, but currently includes:

Jason Buck, John Buck, Douglas Mitchell-Burns, Ruth Butler, Heather Crisp, Isobel Hall, Julian Hight, Peter Horne, James Kinnear, Karen Kinnear, Tina Leary, David Marsh, Sue Molloy, Kate Rotondetto, Dean Scource, Eliza Sackett, Terence Sackett, Sandra Sampson, Adrian Sanders, Sandra Sanger, Julia Skinner, Lewis Taylor, Shelley Tolcher and Lorraine Tuck.